The Digging Badger

Kathryn A. Minta

A SKYLIGHT BOOK

Illustrated with photographs

DODD, MEAD & COMPANY

New York

For Steve

PHOTOGRAPH CREDITS

Charles D. Coppedge, 13, 22, 23, 39, 56; Grand Teton National Park, 11, 45; George W. Frame, 51; Richard Lampe, 52; John P. Messick, 4, 37, 41. All other photographs are by Steve and Kathy Minta.

1   2   3   4   5   6   7   8   9   10

Library of Congress Cataloging in Publication Data

Minta, Kathryn A.
  The digging badger.

  (A Skylight book)
  Includes index.
    1. Badger, American—Juvenile literature.   2. Badgers—
Juvenile literature.   3. Mammals—North America—
Juvenile literature.   I. Title.
QL737.C25M56   1985   599.74′447   85-4353
ISBN 0-396-08654-3

Contents

The North American Badger

A badger is a remarkable digging animal. It digs a burrow to live in. It will dig a burrow to escape an enemy. Mother badgers dig dens for their babies, and that den may be as much as eight feet below ground level. Badgers dig for food, since favorite meals are burrowing rodents. And the badger is speedy about its digging. It is able to dig down six feet or more in only minutes.

The North American badger, known by the scientific name of *Taxidea taxus*, is the only badger that lives on our continent. There are other kinds of badgers throughout the world, and they will be introduced later. But this book is mostly about the North American badger. My

A North American badger appears to be almost as wide as it is tall.

husband, Steve, is a biologist who is completing a study of the North American badger. He designed his study to contribute to the overall knowledge about carnivore ecology. Badgers are carnivores. Like the bear, coyote, bobcat, otter, raccoon, and other carnivores, badgers prey on other animals for food. Knowing how and why badgers do what they do adds to our knowledge of the ecology—the relationship of animals to their environment.

The North American badger lives in the deserts, plains, mountains, and farmlands from southern Canada to southern Mexico and from the Pacific Ocean to as far east as Ohio. The badger seems small because its legs are short and stout, but when fully grown, a large male badger can weigh up to 30 pounds. Most badgers weigh 8 to 26 pounds, are 16 to 28 inches long, and have short fluffy tails. A badger is almost as wide as it is tall. Male badgers are called boars and are larger than the females, which are called sows. Badger babies are born in the spring and are called pups or cubs.

Although both front and back legs are used for digging, a badger's front legs are the most powerful. Its front claws

An average underground burrow is about three feet deep. The dirt thrown out by the badger while digging forms this mound.

can be an inch long and are very thick, while the back claws are only about ³/₈ inch long. When digging, the badger uses its forceful front legs and strong claws to break ground like a shovel. Its less-powerful rear legs and smaller claws are used to scoop, kick, and throw dirt out of the way. As if performing a well-practiced dance step, the badger digs with one foot and kicks dirt behind with the opposite. This right and left, left and right, step is done so rapidly that dirt flies and piles up quickly. No wonder some refer to the badger as the digging machine.

"Fearless" is a term used by some to describe the badger. Once cornered, it has been known to scare off enemies much larger than itself. The badger has a gripping bite. Its jaws are hinged and can lock shut when it bites down on a prey or enemy. This jaw is full of strong and sharp teeth and together they create a vicious and oftentimes fatal wound. A badger can sharpen its own canine teeth just by wearing them. The upper and lower canines form a "canine shear," and the simple action of the bottom canines rubbing the top ones keeps these teeth razor sharp. The canine shear assures that even an old badger will

The badger's front claws are long and sharp and used to break the soil. Its back claws are short and thin, good for kicking and scooping up dirt.

have sharp teeth. But even though it can fight off almost any attacker, if given a choice, a badger would rather dig its way out of danger.

When a badger is aboveground, it moves slowly. Since it appears to be small in size, another predator might easily confuse the badger with a smaller animal and attempt to attack it. However, the bold display of white against the dark coloring of the badger's fur serves as a

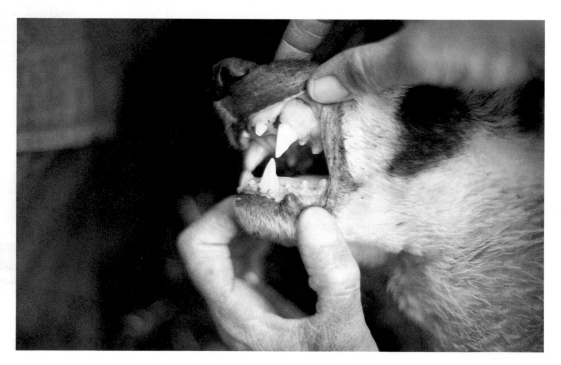

An adult badger has 34 teeth, with canines that are more than ¹/₂ inch long. If cornered, the badger will use its ripping bite to fight off an attacker.

warning to its enemies. Like a skunk, the badger has a white stripe which begins at its nose and continues down its back. The sides of a badger's face are also sharply colored, with white patches on dark fur. Predators quickly learn that these contrasting colors mean an animal with a surprise defense. The badger's surprise is an unexpectedly ferocious defense from a seemingly small and clumsy animal. No predator can afford to risk getting

It may look small and clumsy above the ground, but a badger's warning coloration advertises a surprise defense.

injured, so often a warning such as this is all that is needed to prevent an attack.

A badger's hearing is excellent and its sense of smell is second only to that of dogs. A badger needs to hear and smell better than most animals because it must be able to detect its prey under the ground, especially when hunting burrowing ground squirrels, gophers, and mice. Like a dog, the badger also uses its keen sense of smell to communicate with other badgers. You have probably noticed how a dog sniffs the ground where another dog has been and, after sniffing, will often leave its own scent in that same place. Scientists call this "scent marking," and animals learn much about each other from odors. Like a skunk, the badger has a scent gland from which it emits a musk odor. Unlike the skunk, the badger cannot cover its enemy with this stinky fluid, but the smell is offensive to humans and you would not want to get it on you.

By smelling the scent of another badger, a badger can learn if it was sick or healthy, male or female, and even whether it was a neighbor or a stranger. Scientists are

This badger is standing high on its front legs to look outside its burrow. It can disappear into the ground in seconds.

just beginning to learn more about scent marking through their studies. They have a tough job because we humans smell so poorly, compared to most other mammals. The badger and the dog rely on their sense of smell as much as humans rely on their sense of sight.

I would call you lucky if you were able to sneak up on a badger without it smelling or hearing you first. It may let you watch if you are quiet and stay downwind, but if you get too close, underground it will go. The

North American badger is the fastest digger of any known mammal, and can disappear in no time. If several men with shovels tried to capture a digging badger, it would be surprising if they could catch up with it.

The badger is a nocturnal animal, being most active at night in the cool, moist hours of darkness. Some nocturnal animals—and the badger is one—enjoy daytime play and hunting when the weather is right. Scientists have found that, like most nocturnal animals, the badger does not see in color but is good at seeing shades and forms when light is poor. Its vision is better at night than during daylight hours. The structure of the eye required to let the badger see well with low light does not allow it to see in color.

A badger is never boring to watch. It has an attractive face which can change expressions. When angry, it will curl back its nose and rise up high on its front legs while growling and hissing. If alerted, it will stare intently in your direction. But when curious, playful, or just lazy, it can look very charming. All of this can make badger watching a very special event. It is important to be still

You can't get this close to a badger in the wild. This large male was tranquilized so that an eartag could be put on.

while watching any wild animal. Many animals, including the badger, can see forms much better when there is movement. If you ever spot a badger from a distance it would be best to wait for it to return underground before walking any closer. If you don't wait, the badger may throw a plug of dirt up from underground to block the entrance to its burrow and remain underground for sev-

eral hours or more. You must be sure to approach from downwind, and once you get closer, quietly squat down in the grass or behind a bush, and be still. Then all you can do is hope that when its head pops out you are not noticed. Always remember to be patient because wild animals are not in a hurry and have a much different time clock than humans.

Watching a badger sunbathe can be a lot of fun. A badger out in the warm sun reminds me of a gentle puppy or kitten at play. The badger's fur coat can vary in color from a yellowish brown to a silver gray. Its fur is long, thick, and shaggy, for shedding water and soil. To keep from overheating while resting in the sun it will first dig up some fresh cool soil. After plopping its tummy down to rest in this fresh soil, it suddenly looks like a flat long-furred rug. If it gets too warm, in only a few seconds this digger will turn over more cool soil and rest once again. All badgers look and play a little differently. They may roll around in the dirt, shake, scratch, yawn, and on a bright cool day lie belly-up, really soaking up the sun's rays. When you watch a badger play you would hardly think it would ever harm anything.

· 2 ·
Research
on Badgers

For the last three years my biologist husband, Steve, has been studying the North American badger. We have been researching the large population of badgers that live on the National Elk Refuge in Jackson, Wyoming. The main purpose of the Refuge is to provide range, forage, and feed for an average wintering herd of 7,000 elk. During the winter months you can see a wonderland of wildlife, including elk, bison, coyotes, bald eagles, and many other animals. Elk management is a full-time job, but the Refuge employees were very willing to help us learn more about badgers. I enjoyed living on the Refuge and helping Steve with his fieldwork, and have learned much about badgers from my experience.

A professional biologist does much more than just field-work. It takes years of schooling to set up a well-designed research project. Objectives—what he intends to learn—and methods—the ways in which he collects and analyzes the information—must be clearly outlined and reviewed by other biologists before any actual fieldwork can begin. Steve had to be up-to-date on all that is known about badgers and many other related fields.

Years ago, when very little was known about most

animals except overall descriptions, biologists were often referred to as "naturalists." They were the first to collect and record information about animals in their natural state, and gathering that information took years of pioneering work. As more became known about an animal, questions began to arise about the relationship of the animal to its environment. This more complex area of biology is called "ecology." Much of any biological fieldwork done today is ecological—trying to determine how a particular animal fits into the overall picture.

As an ecological study, Steve has tried to find out why badgers do what they do when they do it, and how they interact with their prey and with each other. For these reasons he must closely follow an individual badger's daily movements. Information from that research will help other biologists who study carnivores, as well as land owners and managers who may need to control the numbers of badgers.

The first step of the fieldwork is to trap as many badgers as possible, so that they can be tagged and followed. At times we have had 34 trap sets—two traps baited and

During the winter months, elk and bison live on the National Elk Refuge.

19

covered with dirt—spread out over 4,000 acres of land. During three trapping seasons we captured a total of 66 different badgers and made 31 recaptures. By using thickly padded traps which hold the badger by a leg, few are harmed while in a trap. Once trapped, a special capture noose is used which slips around the badger's stout neck and locks harmlessly. Your local dogcatcher may use this same type of noose to catch stray dogs. Badgers have long, sharp teeth and claws, and such loose skin that when their fur is gripped they can almost turn around inside their own skin to bite the attacker. Grabbing a badger at the neck is just grabbing a handful of skin.

With the noose around its neck, we give the badger a shot which puts it to sleep for a short time. Badgers can be ferocious when cornered. No one should ever attempt to capture a wild badger unless they have the training, equipment, and experience to do so. In the wild, a sleeping badger is the only safe badger to handle.

Once trapped, each badger will react in a unique way. Some may bury themselves while others dig out huge craters. Often they become "trap wise." Sometimes very

A padded leghold trap set before dirt has been sifted over the traps to conceal them.

A capture noose is locked harmlessly around the badger's neck.

funny things can happen if you catch the same badger more than once. One day Steve recaptured a badger and, just as he did on the first capture, approached her with the noose. She quickly dug a hole and put her nose in it, looking sideways at Steve. Steve was confused until he realized that this badger had learned a new trick. How could he slip the noose over her nose while it was buried? He did manage to get her, but it was much harder the

Once it was asleep, Steve could safely handle this badger.

second time around. We laughed at how this badger had tried to outsmart him.

Once we have a badger safely asleep with a tranquilizer, we weigh it in a burlap sack. The average badger weight was 16 pounds. The largest badger we captured weighed 31 pounds. Because he was so large I named him Big Guy. The badger is examined for scars, wounds, parasites, or diseases. Most of the badgers we captured

were healthy, but if they were not we would give them a shot of penicillin to speed their recovery. Next, measurements are taken of the length of the body, paws, ears, and tail. We pull a small tooth which we send to a laboratory where biologists can count annual tooth rings to find out how old the badger is. The oldest badger of our study was 14 years, which is very old for any badger. Most do not live past six years of age. A numbered eartag is then attached, which assigns each badger its own number so that it can be identified.

Steve was trained by a veterinarian to surgically implant a small radio transmitter inside the body of a badger. This surgery takes approximately 30–45 minutes and the badger is ready to return home in only a couple of hours. Radio-collars are the most common type of transmitter used by wildlife researchers, and because they wrap around the neck of an animal they do not require surgery. But a badger's neck is thicker than its head and collars could easily slide off or, in some cases, become caught in a burrow, causing harm to the badger. For this reason it is better to use implants in studying badgers. Each badger

When Big Guy was released after surgery, he turned back toward our white steel holding cage, looked at us as if to ask what happened, hissed, snarled, and took off toward home.

has its own transmitter with a unique radio frequency, so that we can learn where it goes and what it does by radio-tracking. Transmitters are like miniature radio stations which broadcast the same "beep-beep" signal over and over on the badger's own frequency. Only the receiver picks up the "beep-beep." A transmitter is completely soundless. The signal it sends out cannot be heard by the animal at all. We pick up the signal with our receiver and antenna, and can then follow the badger's movements.

Radio-tracking is best understood if you pretend you are on the Refuge doing it with us. Standing on a butte overlooking the study area, we begin to look for each badger's location. We have 30 badgers with transmitters and they have frequencies numbered 1–30. Turning our receiver to number 1, we listen for a signal—nothing, so number 1 is not around. We continue to search and when the receiver is on number 5 we hear "beep-beep-beep." There it is! By rotating the antenna, we determine its direction and then move to another butte and find its direction from there. Remembering its direction on the first butte, we compare it to the direction from the second butte and calculate its location. Continuing, we get number 7 and the signal is very loud and clear. That means that badger number 7 is close, because the closer you are, the louder the signal sounds. By homing in on the signal with a hand-held antenna we find that badger's exact burrow. By listening very closely to shifts in the rhythm and volume of a signal you can also tell if the badger is active or resting. You can see how valuable radio-tracking is. You can find an animal without ever

For radio-telemetry work, Steven needs a receiver, earphones, and antenna.

seeing it, you do not disturb it, but can even tell if it is active. By using the large antenna on our truck we have gotten locations on badgers which have been as far as five miles away.

Scientists have found that eartags and transmitters are good ways to keep track of an individual animal. But to me each one of our badgers has something special about it, so I also name each badger after one of my favorite people. One of our badgers is named Daisy, and she really moves around. Bob seems to always be hunting, and Robin sticks close to home.

Now that we have detailed information about each badger and can locate the individuals and trace their movements, we concentrate our efforts on the surrounding environment. Climate definitely affects the badger and its movements. Daily records are kept of temperature, wind speed, rain, and snowfall. Snow-tracking is a valuable tool. Because badgers are more active at night, you can get up in the morning and follow badger tracks in the snow from the night before. These tracks tell the story of exactly where the badger went, how many burrows it dug, and where it finally ended up. A badger named Jackie Rose has been tracked for eight miles over snow from one evening of hunting.

Learning what badgers eat is also important. We collect

You can learn a lot of valuable information by snow-tracking animals.

scats (droppings) which are sent to a laboratory for analysis of the diet of the animal at the time that the scat was collected. By estimating the availability of its potential prey (ground squirrels, gophers, mice, and insects) and comparing that with the badger's diet, we can see which type of prey it prefers at what time of the year. We estimate how many fresh burrows are dug and how many old burrows are reused and classify them. We also excavate natal dens (that is, dens where baby badgers are born) after the mother and babies have left for good. We measure, map, and photograph them, in order to learn more about badger life underground.

All of the methods described here are just a quick overview of what a research biologist does when conducting an ecological study. He tries to collect as much information as possible. Doing field research is expensive and going back for additional information is not practical. What is not used for one study may be a great deal of help to another researcher in the future. Once the fieldwork is done, the results must be analyzed and written up in a useful way.

·3·
The Badger's
Family Life

Adult badgers live and hunt alone except during the breeding season. While hunting, a badger is constantly digging to reach its prey, but these burrows also serve as ready-made homes. A badger may stay in the same burrow for days at a time when hunting in a favorite area or it may have a different burrow every day. But over a large portion of its life, a badger concentrates its activities in an area it knows well. Scientists call this area a "home range." A badger is most familiar with its own home range and knows who its neighbors are, where the food is, and where to escape to a nearby burrow if threatened.

To survive, animals must adjust to the weather and

the changing seasons. The easiest seasons for a badger are spring, summer, and fall. The first part of April is the best time of year for a female badger to give birth. In the months to come she will have warm weather, easy travel, and plentiful food while raising her young. The best time to breed is before autumn, when once again the weather is mild, food is plentiful, and travel is easy. A badger can cover miles of ground with little trouble while searching for a mate. After the breeding season of late July and early August, all badgers return to their solitary life. They still have the good months of fall to fatten up for winter.

Another way in which badgers can take advantage of good seasons is by what is called "delayed implantation." Growth of the fertilized egg inside the female is delayed until after the hard months of winter. Then, when the mother badger is not under such hardship, the embryos begin to grow and the babies are born in the spring when life is easier. After growth starts, it takes about five weeks before the young are born. Other mammals, such as bears, also have the advantage of delayed implantation.

A natal den has more than twice the amount of dirt thrown outside than does a regular burrow.

The sow badger will have one to four pups born in an underground home. A burrow where pups are raised is called a natal den. You can often tell the difference between a regular burrow and a den by the amount of dirt thrown on the mound outside the entrance. Dens have more than twice as much dirt outside. The sow badger does her best building when she digs or remodels a den. She wants a safe home with plenty of room for her family.

Badger pups are blind and helpless their first month of life. They are born with pup fur and develop an adult

coat during their first summer. Mother badgers take good care of their pups, keeping them in the safety of a large and deep den. Other animals and humans are not allowed to see them underground. Dr. Hank Harlow at the University of Wyoming has raised badger pups in a laboratory. He has learned a great deal about the growth of pups from his studies. Scientists like Steve are trying to find out more about badgers growing up in the wild, but it would be much easier if they could see more of their underground life.

The mother badger chooses her den before the pups are born. She may not always dig a new den, but decide to reuse an old one. Some dens are reused for years or even decades by many different females. If she chooses an old den she will dig it clean and modify it to her needs. Natal dens can be eight feet deep with many complicated tunnels, chambers, and turnarounds. There is plenty of room for a badger family to be raised in comfort. Of course, one of the most important things to the expectant mother is the safety of her den. Natal dens are often found in areas of thick brush or on a steep out-of-the-

This is a used natal den which we had just started to excavate. Droppings found in natal dens reveal what the pup badgers eat.

way slope. By choosing such a location, the den is less likely to be detected by other predators. The mother prefers not to move her den until her pups have opened their eyes and emerged to the surface. But if the den is threatened by a predator, becomes too dirty with urine or droppings, or food is scarce, she will move to another. If her pups are too young to walk, she will carry them to the new den one at a time.

Full-grown badgers have few natural enemies but, like most animal babies, badger pups have many enemies. A pup cannot dig well until it is around 60 days old. Until then it is too young and too small to fight off an attacker and cannot quickly dig a new burrow or extend the den to escape. So for the first two months of her pups' lives, the mother badger must be very careful. There is evidence that adult badgers that are strangers will eat another badger's pups. Other enemies of badger pups are coyotes, hawks, eagles, and man.

Because the pups are born so small (weighing only ounces) and helpless, the mother must nurse her young and keep them warm an enormous amount of time. She

A young badger pup in Idaho. This one is old enough to venture outside the den.

must groom them and also keep the den as clean as possible. Baby badgers never leave the den at the young, tiny stage. But still she must hunt for a living. For the first four to six weeks, the mother spends less than half the night out hunting for food. She must be very careful

and leaves the den as little as possible. Soon the larger pups need more and more milk and also begin eating solid food. She must now spend more time going farther to keep up with this new demand. Somehow she communicates to her pups that they must not leave the safety of the den when she is away. They must stay underground the entire time she is gone.

Once a baby badger begins to open its eyes, at about 30 days of age, it is probably attracted to the light, and you may soon see them first emerge to the surface. I have watched wild badger pups after their eyes are opened and they come outside with the mother. They love to play, but for many weeks are allowed out only when she is home and only after she gives an "all clear" signal. At times they move quickly, chasing and biting each other. while popping in and out of the den. You often see them rubbing the underside of each other's jaws and necks in a playful snuggle. Pups have a lot of energy and are curious about their new world. I have seen pups pop their heads out of the den to see who I was, but they would not come out onto the mound because the mother

A pup about 30 days old when first emerging from the den.

was away. I wish I could see what they were doing under there. You can hear grunts and scratching, but the rest you just have to imagine. When a badger pup barks, it sounds like a hoarse cough, and when angry or disturbed it will hiss and snarl.

Just imagine being a mother badger coming home after a night of hunting and being greeted by playful pups. After feeding her pups she probably wants to sleep, but

they want to play. She will play in an affectionate way, but when she has had enough and wants to sleep, she can quickly show who is boss.

As the pups get older, the mother teaches them more and more about how to survive life as a badger. Gradually the pups wander farther and farther from the den mound in their play and at two months have made a network of trampled paths. About this time they make their first big digging attempts on the surface. They will practice digging around the den and soon will start to take short trips away from the den with their mother. Their first real journey out into the big world is when the mother begins changing dens. Sticking close to her side, the family moves to a new area. Soon the whole family travels and hunts together. Before late summer the mother must teach her pups a lot, since her family will break up before or during the breeding season at the end of summer.

The pups are three to four months old when the family breaks up. Most badger pups will not breed during their first year of life. When a male suitor comes around to visit the mother, a male pup may be viewed as a com-

A mother and her two-month-old pups were eartagged by John Messick in Idaho.

petitor and will be driven away by the adult male. The mother herself may become cranky toward her female pups. She may just decide to stop sharing her food. So during the breeding season the pups are either driven off by a male badger, not fed, or decide to leave on their own. After the young leave the mother, they may stick together for a short time. But soon each member of the family goes its own way to live the solitary life that badgers prefer.

· 4 ·
The Badger's
Hunting and Food

A badger can live in places which have very different climates. The badger does well from the deserts of Mexico to the sageland mountains of Wyoming to the cool Canadian prairies. A badger's burrow is a great refuge from dry heat and is also good for escaping extreme cold. Burrows vary in depth, but the average one is probably three feet deep.

Badgers survive long, cold winters by taking winter naps, which scientists call "torpor." Animals that hibernate are in a similar state, but hibernation is a much longer and deeper sleep. The badger wakes up from a torpor to hunt during warmer winter days and nights;

One of our badgers awakened from a torpor to hunt a hibernating ground squirrel in several feet of snow.

hibernators will continue to sleep right through until spring. During a period of torpor the badger's heart rate and body temperature slow down. When the weather temperatures increase, the badger's heart rate and body temperature speed up again. The badger then wakes up and goes outside to check the winter conditions. If favorable, it hunts through the snow, returning to nap when conditions are too tough. Badgers can afford long

periods of winter torpor because during autumn abundant food allows them to fatten up. With its heartbeat and body temperature slowed down, this fat can keep the badger warm and it does not have to hunt as much. The longest period that one of our badgers remained in a torpor was 80 days.

Favorite meals of the North American badger are burrowing rodents: prairie dogs, ground squirrels, mice, and gophers. The badger uses its excellent senses of smell and hearing to find a rodent's burrow and exactly where the rodent is located in its underground tunnel system. Once a rodent is located, the badger quickly digs down to capture the prey. It may have to dig in several spots before cornering the prey. Because the badger is quick and has a ripping bite, it has no problem in catching the rodent under the ground. Badgers are perfect at this type of hunting and can dig out several burrows during a single night or day of hunting. If really hungry, one badger can dig up a large area, leaving it full of burrows.

Coyotes and badgers are often seen hunting ground squirrels together. Squirrels often have more than one

Marmots are the largest ground squirrels, some weighing more than 15 pounds. Since they often live in rocky areas, they are harder for badgers to dig out, but they still do it.

entrance to a burrow and while a badger is digging, the squirrels sometimes flee from it by running out of another entrance. The coyote is much faster on the ground than the badger, so it can easily run down the escaping squirrel. If the squirrel does not run out, because it is afraid of the coyote, the badger benefits. But if the squirrel panics and runs because of the badger, the coyote benefits. That is why we may see coyotes and badgers traveling close to each other. Pairs have even been seen resting side by side.

Badgers are super hunters. They change the way they hunt to match the food that is available. Badgers will even kill and eat rattlesnakes. They will root for insects, rob ground nests for bird eggs, catch frogs, and have even been seen fishing for carp at the edge of a shallow lake. They will eat almost anything, continually adapting to changes in available prey to survive.

If food becomes hard to find, a badger will often pick up and leave an area. A badger can swim, so not even water can stop its move in search of better hunting. One of the badgers we studied swam through the large rapidly moving Snake River in Wyoming. He seems to like his new home because he is still there after two years of tracking him. A badger does not need to live near water like some animals do. It does not drink water because it gets the moisture it needs from the foods it eats. This is another reason why badgers can live in dry deserts. However, a friend told me that she had a wild badger that used to enjoy swimming in her swimming hole. Of course, she always waited to begin her swim until the badger was finished.

·5·
Badger
Relatives

Badgers have been around for many millions of years, and the North American badger looks and acts much the same now as it did at least three million years ago.

Scientists have classified badgers in the order Carnivora. Members of this order are very different from each other in both size and shape. The smallest carnivore, the least weasel, weighs only one or two ounces. The largest, the Alaskan brown bear, can weigh as much as 1,500 pounds. But they all have one thing in common—they are mammals that hunt other animals for food.

Some of the most primitive of the meat-eaters or carnivores are members of the family Mustelidae, to which the badgers belong. The name Mustelidae comes from a word which means "musk." Musk is a strong odor and is what a skunk sprays when it wants to be left alone. Badgers and their family members all have musk. In some species it is stronger than in others and is used as a defense.

There are nine badger species that live in different places almost throughout the world. Each has the common name "badger" and they are all diggers.

The least weasel is the smallest carnivore, weighing only one or two ounces. This one was collected for a museum specimen.

THE EUROPEAN BADGER *(Meles meles)*

The name tells you where it is found—in a large area of Europe—but it is also found in the cooler parts of Asia. This badger digs burrows which are called sets (or setts). These sets are like underground castles, sometimes two or three stories deep. Badger watching is a popular pastime in England. European badgers are fun to watch because they live together in extended family groups called clans. When together, they have been seen many times playing the badgers' version of leapfrog and king of the mountain. Strangely, in many places such as England, this badger's favorite food is earthworms. It also eats rabbits, mice, grubs, slugs, snails, and insects.

THE HOG BADGER *(Arctonyx collaris)*

The hog badger likes a warm climate and lives in tropical forest lands, including most of Asia. This badger has a long piglike snout which is good for rooting; its claws are nearly white. Like a hog, it uses its snout to root out its favorite foods, such as insects, plants, worms, and reptile eggs. Scientists know little about this badger because it is shy and rarely seen.

The Honey Badger (*Mellivora capensis*)

Many know this ferocious badger that lives in Africa, the Middle East, and India, and call it by another name, the ratel. It is better left alone, since it is very aggressive. When in pairs, honey badgers can kill animals much larger than themselves. This badger can also climb trees. It hunts birds, rodents, and even the dangerous cobra. It also hunts in cooperation with a bird, the honeyguide. Both bird and badger like to eat honey, wax, and bee larvae. When the honeyguide locates a hive, it makes calls at a nearby badger and the badger quickly follows the bird to the honey tree. The badger seems unharmed by the bee stings and climbs the tree and digs out the hive. The badger rarely eats everything, so the bird and badger both benefit. This badger is a real scavenger. In India it has been seen robbing human graves in search of edible flesh.

Stink Badgers (*Mydaus javanensis* and *Mydaus marchei*)

Can it stink? Most definitely, yes. Whenever attacked or frightened, the stink badger will raise its tail like

The honey badger, or ratel, is one of the most ferocious carnivores. This one was photographed by Dr. George W. Frame in Tanzania.

a skunk and spray its enemy. When sprayed into the eyes of a dog, it has been known to blind them. This badger even looks somewhat like a skunk, with a broad band of white down its back. Little is known about it because it lives in remote areas of Borneo, Java, and Sumatra. We do know it eats worms, bird eggs, and tiny animals. This badger has been seen sharing its burrow with the barbed porcupine, which must be of some mutual benefit to both.

FERRET BADGERS (*Melogale moschata, Melogale personata,* and *Melogale everetti*)

The smallest and best tree climber of all badgers, the ferret badger moves quickly, and has short fur and a long bushy tail. It is quick both in the trees and on the ground. It eats small animals, eggs, reptiles, insects, fruit, and berries. At times it is welcomed into the homes of humans because it eats insect pests. This badger lives in Asia, mostly in eastern China, Java, and Borneo.

· 6 ·
Badgers
as Pets

Badgers can make great pets. I have talked with people who have raised badgers and they all say they would like to have another one. It is strange that the tough badger, when raised by humans, can be so tame. A badger captured when full-grown would not be a good pet at all. You must raise one from a pup, and it is even better if its eyes are not yet opened. A pet badger will follow its owner around and will even ride in cars and trucks. I read a newspaper article about a pet badger that became a well-known occupant of its owner's grocery store. Another friend told me that he took his badger to football games on a leash.

Opposite: The ferret badger's long tail helps in balancing while climbing. Photo taken by Richard Lampe at the National Provincial Museum in Taipei, Taiwan.

One problem all badger owners have is trying to keep their pets out of the yard and garden. If you own a badger you must be willing to fill in a lot of holes. Trying to keep a badger inside a house can also be quite frustrating because of the musk odor (badger smell) and its need to scratch and chew.

Henrietta was my pet badger and she was probably about 30 days old when I first got her. We found her injured on the Refuge. I remember how surprised I was when she started to snuggle. She loved to be cuddled and liked rubbing her face against mine. After I would feed her she would rub her neck on my cheeks and neck, and nuzzle her way into a warm spot to sleep. If I was holding her while lying down, she would fall asleep on my chest. Like all badgers, she loved to dig, though at her age she mostly just pushed dirt around. To keep her comfortable, I gave her a small ice chest and filled one-half of it with dirt. She was so cute to watch. Once she got started, dirt would fly out of that small cooler. She yawned and slept a lot but at night when I wanted to sleep, she did not. Playing tug-of-war with a rag was an

Henrietta in her dirt-filled ice chest

all-time favorite. If for some reason she was unhappy, she could really let you know by snarling and barking. When badgers snarl, they sound like a person snoring very loudly in bursts. When Henrietta barked, it sounded more like a hoarse cough.

We hoped that once Henrietta's injuries had healed, we could return her to the mother badger. After she had been treated by a veterinarian, we ourselves gave her constant care for five weeks. She seemed to be improving, wanting to play and snuggle, scratch at the dirt, eat and

bark more every day. But suddenly her little body gave up and could no longer fight the stress of being injured at such a young age. Although we knew that people arc oftcn not successful at raising very young wild animals, we were heartbroken when Henrietta died. Almost everyone who saw her wanted her, but even if she were not injured, I could not have givėn her away.

You can learn a lot by raising a wild animal, but you do not learn what the animal is really like if it were raised by its own mother and allowed to remain wild. Humans,

no matter how they try, cannot replace what an animal mother can teach her young.

Some badgers never make good pets, while others do. Many are good for a short time and then become problems for their owners and are no longer happy. Then the owner faces the question of what to do with a badger that was never taught by its mother how to survive in the wild on its own. Only in special circumstances does it seem fair to raise a wild animal as a pet. In most cases, it is probably selfish of humans to try.

Young Henrietta liked to snuggle.

· 7 ·
People
and Badgers

Has anyone ever said to you, "Don't badger me"? If you have ever seen a bothered badger, you would surely not want to be badgered. Badgers are tough and will not back down. As a matter of fact, a definition of the verb "to badger" is to tease, bait, worry, or pester.

Many years ago, lead miners in the state of Wisconsin were nicknamed badgers. Badgerlike, these pioneers dug homes for themselves in the hillsides and were able to live through the many hardships of early settlement life.

Some think that the dark markings on a badger's face look like a badge and that its name was derived from this common word. Others believe that the name "badger" came from the French word *"becheur,"* meaning a digger. The badger has a nickname given to it by the Mexican Indians. They called it "Talcoyote," which means "like a coyote," because badgers and coyotes are often seen hunting together.

Badgers have been used by man for hundreds of years. During the seventeenth century in Europe, some people believed that badgers had magical powers. These people collected their furs and claws, so that they could have some of the badgers' magic. Scottish kilts were decorated with a badger's fur and head, which was made into a pouch. In England, badger and dog fights were a favored sport at one time. This was called badger baiting. Several dogs and a badger were placed in a pit together. Only some would live through the fight and it was a bloody, cruel sport. Badgers were also chased down and hunted. Thank goodness, badger watching is now more popular than badger fighting.

The badger is considered by many to be a pest, even though badgers help control rodent populations. Ranchers fear that livestock may step into a badger burrow and break a leg. Farmers become angry when their equipment runs into holes and mounds or when irrigation water is misdirected because of a badger burrow. People who feel the badger is a pest will kill it by shooting, trapping, or poisoning. Some will pour water down the burrow until the badger surfaces and then kill it.

Badger fur has some value to man. Today, some people like badger coats and, because badger fur is the best water shedder, it is used for paint and shaving brushes. A painter's brush made from badger fur is called a "badger."

The skin of a badger is so tough that it is used for making drumheads, gloves, and shoes. Strangely enough, the scent gland of a stink badger has been used to make perfume. Badgers are not often used for food because the meat is strong-tasting and oily.

Despite its reputation for ferocity, many have loved the badger. Mr. Badger is a main character in Kenneth Grahame's book, *The Wind in the Willows.* Have you ever read about Mr. Badger? There are also delightful stories about Frances the badger by Russell Hoban. Several schools call their athletic teams the Badgers, but the people of Wisconsin probably love the badger the most. They even refer to their state as the "Badger State." The badger is the official state animal in Wisconsin. No one would dare have a badger-dog fight there. The University of Wisconsin has selected Bucky Badger as their symbol. He is on T-shirts, sweaters, mugs, notebooks, towels, dolls, and many other items you can purchase there. In Wisconsin the people are pleased when the badger does well. If someone there called you a badger, that would definitely be a compliment.

An example of how many burrows a population of badgers can dig. They were after a pest, the ground squirrel, but farmers and ranchers do not think the results are worth it.

Badgers, like all other animals, must share their world with mankind. The human population is increasing and the land is constantly being changed for man's uses. We cannot stop this growth and many animals suffer because of it. Some animals do better than others at surviving with man. The North American badger is a good example of a species which has benefited from man's use of open land. Agriculture has increased prey species of squirrels and mice because these animals eat plant crops and seeds. Thus, the badger has an increased food supply. And because the badger can dig anywhere, hiding and denning spots are no scarcer. In fact, since man has begun altering

the continent, the North American badger has spread its range throughout much of North America. No one knows exactly how many North American badgers there are today. Reports from private and government land managers, trappers, and biologists, along with requests from individuals for badger control, all indicate an increase.

Other animals—the grizzly bear, the bald eagle, the bison—have not been as fortunate as the badger. Perhaps in the future man will make wildlife a more important part of his land-use planning. It is impossible to bring back what is gone, but with intelligent planning we can save what we still have. The badger may be doing well now, but we must not assume that, no matter what we do, it always will. When plans for the future are made, all creatures should be considered, even those that live underground like the badger.

Becky and Bucky badger dolls from Wisconsin

Index